100
HARDEST
HITTING
QUOTES

BRITTNEY MADELEN

FOR THOSE DEVOTED TO BETTERING THEMSELVES.

IF ANY OF THESE QUOTES HIT YOU, TEAR IT OUT, FRAM
IT, PUT IT SOMEWHERE YOU CAN SEE IT DAILY.
MOST IMPORTANTLY, APPLY IT.

And the day came when the risk
to remain tight as a bud was
more painful than the risk it
took to blossom

Anais Nin

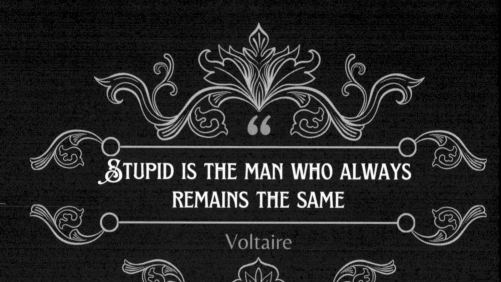

> **STUPID IS THE MAN WHO ALWAYS REMAINS THE SAME**
>
> Voltaire

"Until you value yourself, you won't value your time, Until you value your time, you will not do anything with it.

M. Scott Peck

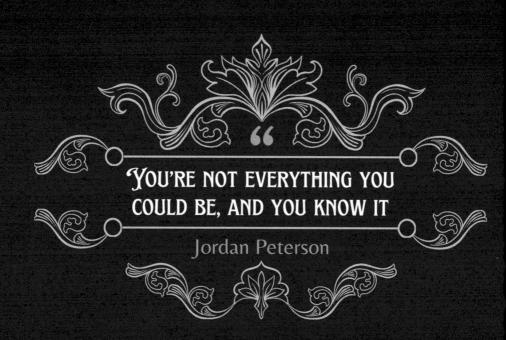

You're not everything you could be, and you know it

Jordan Peterson

LIFE'S UNDER NO OBLIGATION TO
GIVE US WHAT WE EXPECT

Margaret Mitchell

"YOUR PRESENT CIRCUMSTANCES DON'T DETERMINE WHERE YOU CAN GO; THEY MERELY DETERMINE WHERE YOU START

Nido Qubein

THE POSSESSION OF ANYTHING
BEGINS IN THE MIND

Bruce Lee

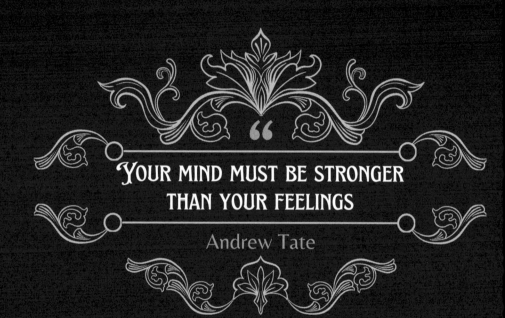

"
YOUR MIND MUST BE STRONGER
THAN YOUR FEELINGS

Andrew Tate

WHETHER YOU THINK YOU CAN OR THINK YOU CAN'T, YOU'RE RIGHT

Henry Ford

RULE YOUR MIND, WHICH, IF IT IS
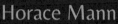NOT YOUR SERVANT, IS YOUR
MASTER

Horace Mann

Any person capable of angering you becomes your master

Epictetus

"

YOU ARE TODAY WHERE YOUR
THOUGHTS HAVE BROUGHT YOU, YOU
WILL BE TOMORROW WHERE YOUR
THOUGHTS TAKE YOU

James Allen

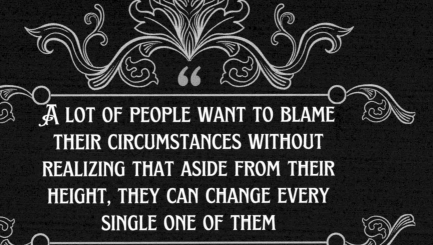

A LOT OF PEOPLE WANT TO BLAME
THEIR CIRCUMSTANCES WITHOUT
REALIZING THAT ASIDE FROM THEIR
HEIGHT, THEY CAN CHANGE EVERY
SINGLE ONE OF THEM

Tristan Tate

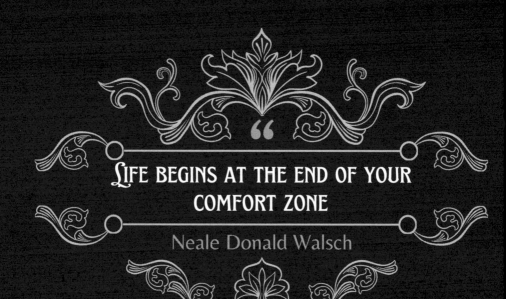

"
LIFE BEGINS AT THE END OF YOUR
COMFORT ZONE

Neale Donald Walsch

IT MAY SEEM DIFFICULT AT FIRST, BUT EVERYTHING IS DIFFICULT AT FIRST

Miyamoto Musashi

Too many of us are not living our dreams because we are living our fears

Les Brown

THERE IS NO GREATER AGONY THAN BEARING AN UNTOLD STORY INSIDE YOU

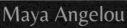

Maya Angelou

WHATEVER YOU'RE MEANT TO DO, DO IT NOW. THE CONDITIONS ARE ALWAYS IMPOSSIBLE

Doris Lessing

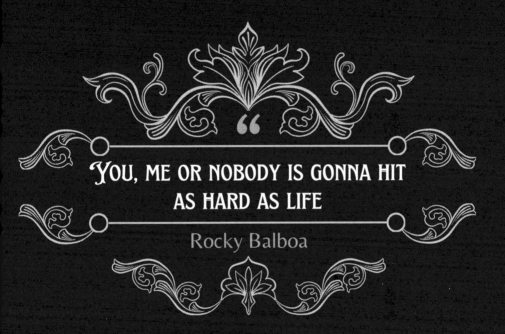

You, me or nobody is gonna hit
as hard as life

Rocky Balboa

"Being challenged in life is inevitable, being defeated is optional"

Roger Crawford

Don't waste a good mistake, learn from it

Robert T. Kiyosaki

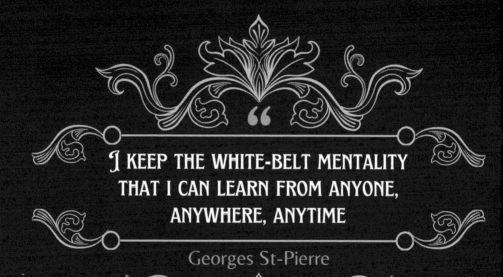

I KEEP THE WHITE-BELT MENTALITY THAT I CAN LEARN FROM ANYONE, ANYWHERE, ANYTIME

Georges St-Pierre

THOSE WHO KEEP LEARNING WILL KEEP RISING IN LIFE

Charlie Munger

SUCCESSFUL PEOPLE HAVE LIBRARIES. THE REST HAVE BIG SCREEN TV'S

Jim Rohn

MORE GOLD HAD BEEN MINED
FROM THE MIND OF MEN THAN THE
EARTH IT SELF

Napolean Hill

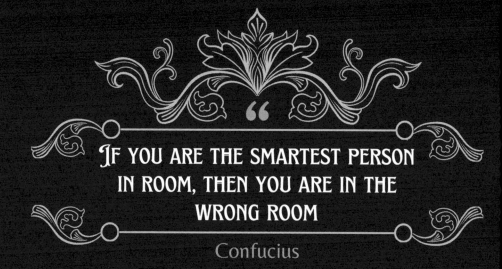

IF YOU ARE THE SMARTEST PERSON
IN ROOM, THEN YOU ARE IN THE
WRONG ROOM

Confucius

 Evil is whatever distracts

Franz Kafka

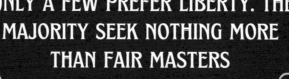

Only a few prefer liberty. The majority seek nothing more than fair masters

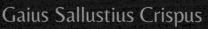

Gaius Sallustius Crispus

It is the business of the very few to be independent; it is a privilege of the strong

Friedrich Nietzsche

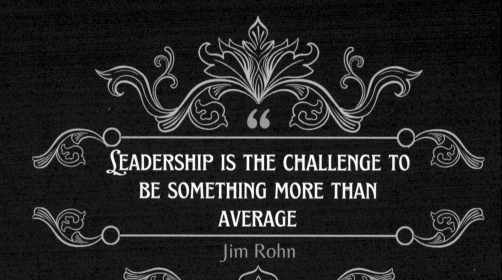

" LEADERSHIP IS THE CHALLENGE TO
BE SOMETHING MORE THAN
AVERAGE

Jim Rohn

> "It's no secret that becoming healthy requires a commitment to exercising- and that means you need to stop being a lazy pu**y

John Joseph

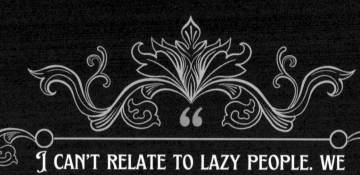

I CAN'T RELATE TO LAZY PEOPLE. WE
DON'T SPEAK THE SAME LANGUAGE. I
DON'T UNDERSTAND YOU. I DON'T
WANT TO UNDERSTAND YOU

Kobe Bryant

Don't stop when you're tired.
Stop when you're done

David Goggins

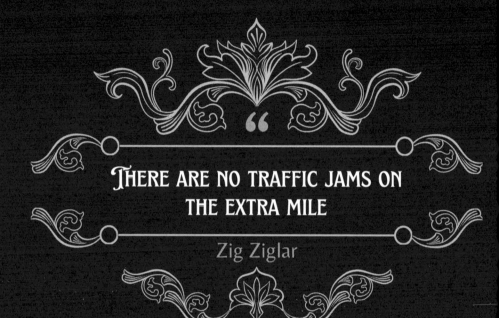

THERE ARE NO TRAFFIC JAMS ON
THE EXTRA MILE

Zig Ziglar

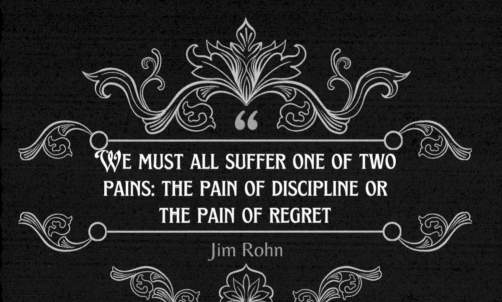

WE MUST ALL SUFFER ONE OF TWO PAINS: THE PAIN OF DISCIPLINE OR THE PAIN OF REGRET

Jim Rohn

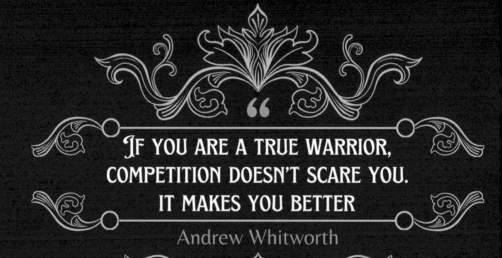

If you are a true warrior, competition doesn't scare you. It makes you better

Andrew Whitworth

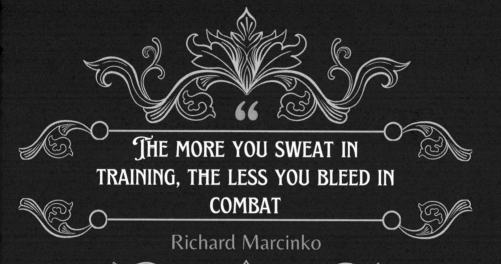

"
THE MORE YOU SWEAT IN
TRAINING, THE LESS YOU BLEED IN
COMBAT

Richard Marcinko

PAIN IS GOOD. TRUE WISDOM
COMES FROM PAIN; PAIN TURNS
FOLLOWERS INTO LEADERS AND
MAKES THE WEAK STRONG

Kwang S. Kim

FATE WHISPERS TO THE
WARRIOR,"YOU CAN NOT WITHSTAND
THE STORM." THE WARRIOR WHISPERS
BACK," I AM THE STORM."

Jake Remington

You'll laugh at your fears
when you find out who you are

Piccolo

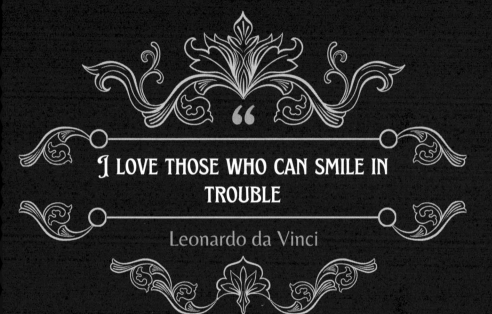

I LOVE THOSE WHO CAN SMILE IN TROUBLE

Leonardo da Vinci

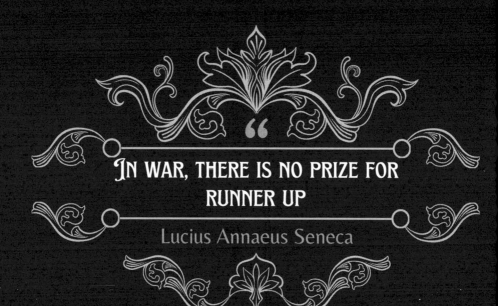

"

IN WAR, THERE IS NO PRIZE FOR
RUNNER UP

Lucius Annaeus Seneca

EVERYTHING HANGS ON ONE'S
THINKING... A MAN IS AS UNHAPPY AS
HE HAS CONVINCED HIMSELF HE IS

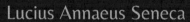

Lucius Annaeus Seneca

"

THERE ARE NO LIMITATIONS TO THE
MIND EXCEPT THOSE WE
ACKNOWLEDGE. BOTH POVERTY AND
RICHES ARE THE OFFSPRING OF
THOUGHT

Napolean Hill

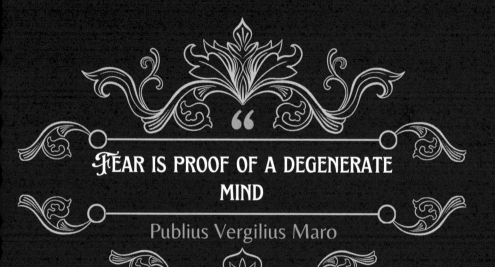

"

Fear is proof of a degenerate mind

Publius Vergilius Maro

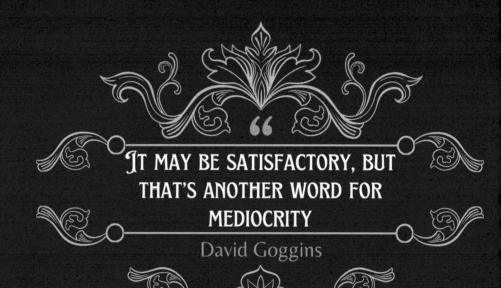

"

IT MAY BE SATISFACTORY, BUT
THAT'S ANOTHER WORD FOR
MEDIOCRITY

David Goggins

MEDIOCRITY DOESN'T JUST HAPPEN.
IT'S CHOSEN OVER TIME THROUGH
SMALL CHOICES DAY BY DAY

Todd Henry

CHOICE, NOT CHANCE DETERMINES YOUR DESTINY

Aristotle

He who dares not offend,
cannot be honest

Thomas Paine

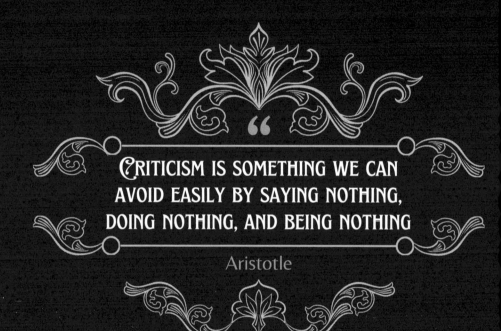

CRITICISM IS SOMETHING WE CAN
AVOID EASILY BY SAYING NOTHING,
DOING NOTHING, AND BEING NOTHING

Aristotle

"YOU CANNOT WISH FOR BOTH
STRONG CHARACTER AND AN EASY
LIFE. THE PRICE OF EACH IS THE
OTHER

Alex Hormozi

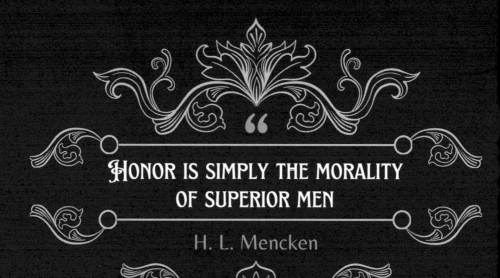

HONOR IS SIMPLY THE MORALITY OF SUPERIOR MEN

H. L. Mencken

ONE OF THE TRUEST TESTS OF INTEGRITY IS ITS BLUNT REFUSAL TO BE COMPROMISED

Chinua Achebe

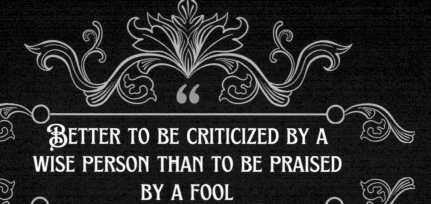

BETTER TO BE CRITICIZED BY A
WISE PERSON THAN TO BE PRAISED
BY A FOOL

Ecclesiastes 7:5

RATHER FAIL WITH HONOR THAN SUCCEED BY FRAUD

Sophocles

Be ashamed to die until you have won some victory for humanity

Horace Mann

ONLY PUT OFF UNTIL TOMORROW
WHAT YOU ARE WILLING TO DIE
HAVING LEFT UNDONE

Pablo Picasso

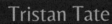

ACCOMPLISHMENT HONORS YOUR ANCESTORS

Tristan Tate

THE TWO MOST IMPORTANT DAYS
IN YOUR LIFE ARE THE DAY YOU
ARE BORN AND THE DAY YOU FIND
OUT WHY

Mark Twain

"I HATED EVERY MINUTE OF TRAINING, BUT I SAID, 'DON'T QUIT. SUFFER NOW AND LIVE THE REST OF YOUR LIFE AS A CHAMPION'

Muhammad Ali

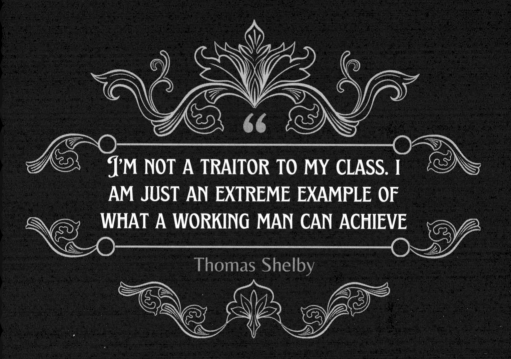

"

I'M NOT A TRAITOR TO MY CLASS. I
AM JUST AN EXTREME EXAMPLE OF
WHAT A WORKING MAN CAN ACHIEVE

Thomas Shelby

"Pain doesn't tell you when you ought to stop. Pain is the little voice in your head that tries to hold you back because it knows if you continue you will change

Kobe Bryant

" WE DON'T DO COMMERCIALS
BECAUSE OUR TARGET AUDIENCE ISN'T
SITTING AROUND WATCHING TV

Lamborghini

THE PRICE OF ANYTHING IS THE
AMOUNT OF LIFE YOU EXCHANGE
FOR IT

Henry David Thoreau

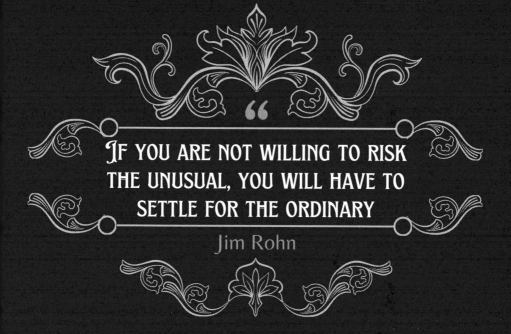

"

If you are not willing to risk
the unusual, you will have to
settle for the ordinary

Jim Rohn

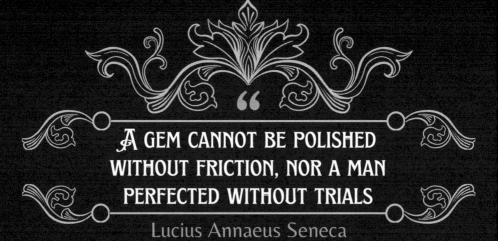

"

A GEM CANNOT BE POLISHED
WITHOUT FRICTION, NOR A MAN
PERFECTED WITHOUT TRIALS

Lucius Annaeus Seneca

Don't fear failure. not failure,
but low aim is the crime. in
great attempts, it is glorious
even to fail

Bruce Lee

Don't set your goals too low, if you don't need much, you won't become much

Jim Rohn

A MAN IS GREAT NOT BECAUSE HE
HASN'T FAILED; A MAN IS GREAT
BECAUSE FAILURE HASN'T STOPPED
HIM

Confucius

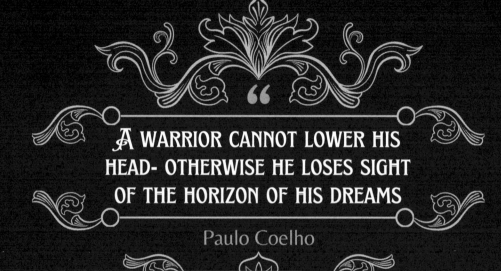

A WARRIOR CANNOT LOWER HIS
HEAD- OTHERWISE HE LOSES SIGHT
OF THE HORIZON OF HIS DREAMS

Paulo Coelho

"

DRIPPING WATER HOLLOWS OUT
STONE, NOT THROUGH FORCE BUT
THROUGH PERSISTENCE

Ovid

Let him who desires peace
prepare for war

Publius Flavius Vegetius Renatus

" THE DAY A MAN BECOMES SUPERIOR TO PLEASURE, HE WILL ALSO BE SUPERIOR TO PAIN

Lucius Anneus Seneca

YOU WON'T ALWAYS BE
MOTIVATED, SO YOU MUST BE
DISCIPLINED

Unknown

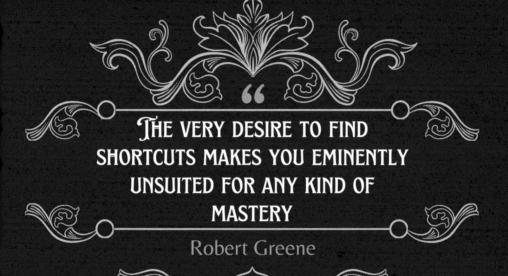

THE VERY DESIRE TO FIND
SHORTCUTS MAKES YOU EMINENTLY
UNSUITED FOR ANY KIND OF
MASTERY

Robert Greene

THE PESSIMIST COMPLAINS ABOUT
THE WIND; THE OPTIMIST EXPECTS
IT TO CHANGE; THE REALIST
ADJUSTS THE SAILS

William Arthur Ward

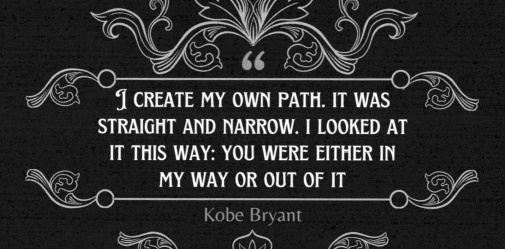

I CREATE MY OWN PATH. IT WAS
STRAIGHT AND NARROW. I LOOKED AT
IT THIS WAY: YOU WERE EITHER IN
MY WAY OR OUT OF IT

Kobe Bryant

WHEN SETTING OUT ON A JOURNEY,
DO NOT SEEK ADVICE FROM THOSE
WHO HAVE NEVER LEFT HOME

Rumi

BEWARE OF THE ADVICE OF ORDINARY MEN, IT BRINGS NOTHING BUT THE ORDINARY

Tristan Tate

EXPECT, WHILE REACHING FOR THE
STARS, PEOPLE TO WHIRL BY WITH
THEIR DARK CLOUDS AND STORM
UPON YOU

Anthony Liccione

When there is no enemy within, the enemies outside cannot hurt you

Winston Churchill

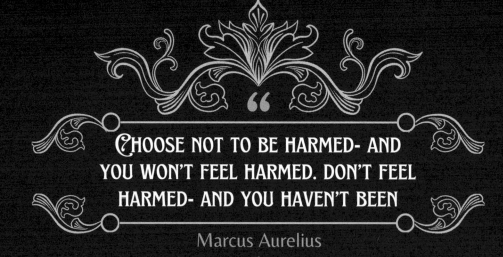

"

CHOOSE NOT TO BE HARMED- AND
YOU WON'T FEEL HARMED. DON'T FEEL
HARMED- AND YOU HAVEN'T BEEN

Marcus Aurelius

 Reject your sense of injury and the injury itself disappears

 Marcus Aurelius

THIS ABOVE ALL, TO REFUSE TO BE A VICTIM

Margaret Atwood

LIFE CONSISTS NOT IN HOLDING
GOOD CARDS BUT IN PLAYING
THOSE YOU HOLD WELL

Josh Billings

CONTINUOUS IMPROVEMENT IS BETTER THAN DELAYED PERFECTION

Mark Twain

LUCK IS WHEN AN OPPORTUNITY
COMES ALONG AND YOU'RE
PREPARED FOR IT

Denzel Washington

I'M A GREAT BELIEVER IN LUCK, AND I FIND THE HARDER I WORK THE MORE I HAVE OF IT

Stephen Leacock

BUT THE GREATEST BATTLE OF ALL IS
WITH YOURSELF- YOUR WEAKNESSES,
YOUR EMOTIONS, YOUR LACK OF
RESOLUTION IN SEEING THINGS THROUGH
TO THE END. YOU MUST DECLARE
UNCEASING WAR ON YOURSELF.

Robert Greene

THE CAVE YOU FEAR TO ENTER
HOLDS THE TREASURE YOU SEEK

Joseph Campbell

A PERSON OFTEN MEETS HIS
DESTINY ON THE ROAD HE TOOK TO
AVOID IT

Jean de La Fontaine

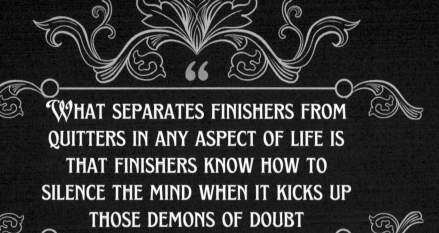

WHAT SEPARATES FINISHERS FROM
QUITTERS IN ANY ASPECT OF LIFE IS
THAT FINISHERS KNOW HOW TO
SILENCE THE MIND WHEN IT KICKS UP
THOSE DEMONS OF DOUBT

John Joseph

"

Most great people have achieved their greatest success just one step beyond their greatest failure

Napoleon Hill

DEVOTE THE REST OF YOUR LIFE TO MAKING PROGRESS

Epictetus

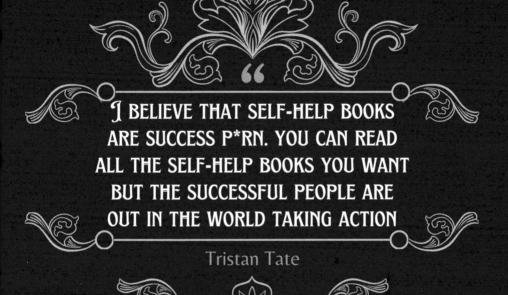

" I BELIEVE THAT SELF-HELP BOOKS
ARE SUCCESS P*RN. YOU CAN READ
ALL THE SELF-HELP BOOKS YOU WANT
BUT THE SUCCESSFUL PEOPLE ARE
OUT IN THE WORLD TAKING ACTION

Tristan Tate

One day you will wake up and there won't be any more time to do things you've always wanted. Do it now

Paulo Coelho

"No such thing as spare time, no such thing as free time, no such thing as down time. All you got is life time. Go

Henry Rollins

IN THE END, WHEN IT'S OVER, ALL
THAT MATTERS IS WHAT YOU'VE DONE

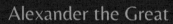

Alexander the Great

TODAY I SHALL BEHAVE AS IF THIS
IS THE DAY I WILL BE REMEMBERED

Dr. Seuss

"

HOW LONG ARE YOU GOING TO WAIT
BEFORE YOU DEMAND THE BEST FOR
YOURSELF?

Epictetus

KEEP IN MIND, WHATEVER YOUR ADVERSITY,
CHALLENGE, HARDSHIP, OR FAILURE..

"KNOW THAT I AM WITH YOU;
YES, TO THE END OF TIME"

-JESUS

"Have I not commanded thee? Be strong and of good courage; be not afraid, neither be thou dismayed: for the Lord thy God is with thee whithersoever thou goest."

Joshua 1:9 KJV

Words from some of the world's legendaries that will ignite the fire within you. Consider this your little black book.

Now go and prosper!

Made in the USA
Columbia, SC
13 November 2024

7289909b-de60-449c-b649-7d497c70bb25R02